EXTREME CAREERS

ASTRONAUTS
Life Exploring Outer Space

Chris Hayhurst

the rosen publishing group's
rosen
central

Published in 2001 by The Rosen Publishing Group, Inc.
29 East 21st Street, New York, NY 10010

First Edition

Library of Congress Cataloging-in-Publication Data

Hayhurst, Chris.
Astronauts : life exploring outer space / by Chris Hayhurst.— 1st ed.
p. cm. — (Extreme careers)
Includes bibliographical references and index.
ISBN 0-8239-3364-4 (library binding)
1. Astronautics—Vocational guidance—Juvenile literature. 2. Astronauts—Juvenile literature. 3. Outer space—Exploration—Juvenile literature. [1. Astronautics—Vocational guidance. 2. Astronauts. 3. Vocational guidance. 4. Outer space—Exploration.] I. Title. II. Series.
TL850 .H39 2001
629.45'023—dc21

00-011956

Manufactured in the United States of America

Contents

Liftoff

T-minus ten . . . nine . . . eight . . . seven . . . six . . . With a deafening roar, the space shuttle's three liquid rocket engines come to life. The ship begins to rock—shaking, vibrating. "We have main-engine start . . . four . . . three . . . two . . . one . . . and liftoff . . . The space shuttle has cleared the tower."

Because of a recent spell of bad weather, the launch of the shuttle has been delayed for days. First it was the threat of rain—even the slightest drizzle can damage the shuttle's heat-resistant tiles when the craft rockets into the sky at more than a thousand miles per hour. Then it was gusty winds, which would have made an emergency landing impossible. Even as late as this morning, the mission could have been canceled at a moment's notice. But a series of elaborate tests and inspections—including an icicle check by the NASA "ice team" and a computer scan of every last inch of the craft— turned up nothing out of the ordinary. From the looks of things, the mission is full speed ahead. It is "all systems go," and as the shuttle rips off the launch pad and into the crisp January sky, the crowd at the Kennedy Space Center in Cape Canaveral, Florida, lets out a cheer.

Aboard the shuttle, the applause goes unnoticed. The engines are so loud, the vibrations so overwhelming, that the crew is doing all it can just to hold on. Glued to their seats by gravitational forces are seven astronauts: the shuttle commander, the pilot, an electrical engineer, an aerospace engineer, a satellite engineer, and two scientists. Strapped down in their protective flight suits, they grip the controls and look up toward space.

In just thirty-five seconds, the ship is well on its way, four miles off the ground and speeding toward

Successful space launches are the culmination of the efforts of many brave individuals, including the astronauts who risk their lives on every mission.

the stars at 1,500 miles per hour. If anything goes wrong, the shuttle can perform an "RTLS"—a return to launch site. The orbiter will drop its attached booster rockets and fuel tank and then swoop back down for an emergency landing.

A few minutes later, the ship's destiny is certain. As the shuttle increases its speed, the astronauts struggle to breathe. Faster and faster, the craft hurtles up and through Earth's atmosphere. Then, suddenly, silence. Darkness. Space.

Space flight might seem routine today, but years ago, just the thought of sending people into space was considered absurd. Space was so far away, so dark, so seemingly dangerous. No one knew what was in space, much less whether humans could survive there. Space was the final frontier—the last truly unexplored territory.

But by the late 1950s, officials in both the United States and the Soviet Union had made up their minds. Space had to be explored. There could be no greater accomplishment, no surer demonstration of technological know-how and power. For both countries, it was a matter of national pride. The race to space was on.

The Right Stuff

1

Just what does it take to become an astronaut? Ask John Glenn.

Glenn is no newcomer to space. Almost forty years ago, on February 20, 1962, Glenn was the first American to orbit Earth. During that solo voyage, in a cramped titanium spacecraft named *Friendship 7*, Glenn circled Earth three times at almost 18,000 miles per hour.

In 1998, at the age of seventy-seven, Glenn returned to space for a second time. Working as a payload specialist aboard the space shuttle *Discovery*, Glenn conducted important experiments for the U.S. National Aeronautics and Space Administration (NASA) and helped scientists on Earth learn how space affects aging and the elderly. Despite his earlier experience, Glenn, a former U.S. senator, had to learn all over again what it takes to be an astronaut.

Things had changed tremendously since those early days of space exploration. Glenn's first trip to space was aboard a craft with just fifty-six control switches, a single window, and thirty-six cubic feet of moving room. *Discovery*, on the other hand, was enormous, almost luxurious in comparison. On his

In February 1962, John Glenn was the first American to orbit Earth.

Race to the Moon

"I believe this nation should commit itself to achieving the goal, before this decade is out, of landing a man on the Moon and returning him safely to Earth. No single space project in this period will be more impressive to mankind, or more important in the long-range exploration of space; and none will be so difficult or expensive to accomplish."
—President John F. Kennedy, May 25, 1961

first journey into space, Glenn's mission was to survive. This time around, survival was pretty much guaranteed. His job was to work.

Types of Astronauts

Successful space flights depend on the collaboration of astronauts with different training and expertise. Pilot astronauts can serve as either the space shuttle commander or as pilot. The commander is responsible for the shuttle, the mission's success, and the safe return of everyone aboard. The pilot's job is to assist the commander in operating the shuttle. Pilots also help deploy and retrieve satellites using the shuttle's mechanical arm, called the remote manipulator system, or RMS.

Another astronaut is the mission specialist. Mission specialists work with the commander and the pilot. Their primary job is to conduct experiments. They also serve as managers of payload operations.

Mission specialists, like astronaut Julie Payette, are responsible for conducting experiments and managing payload operations.

Sometimes they take part in extravehicular activities (EVAs) such as space walks.

The last type of astronaut is the payload specialist. Payload specialists are usually professional scientists brought along to conduct experiments, or technicians familiar with spacecraft equipment. They do not take part in the vigorous training program that other astronauts must endure, but they do go through intensive preparation for their specific mission.

Steps to Success

To be considered for an astronaut position, you have to be qualified. Both mission specialist and pilot astronaut candidates must have a college degree and several years of related work experience. For a mission specialist, that experience might be as a professional scientist familiar with complex laboratory experiments. Pilot candidates should have plenty of experience flying commercial or military jets. It also helps to have a graduate degree. The degree should be in engineering, the biological sciences, the physical sciences, or mathematics. And the

experience—well, let's just say you'd better be good at what you do.

If you decide to apply for a position as a mission specialist, there's one more requirement you'll have to meet: the NASA Class II space physical. Among other things, the physical requires good vision and a healthy blood pressure.

Pilot astronaut applicants have to pass a similar physical, only theirs is known as Class I. They also need at least 1,000 hours of head-pilot flying time in jet aircraft.

If you pass the physical, you'll move on to the next stage—a series of interviews and medical evaluations. Ultimately, a selection

The first U.S. astronaut to fly into orbit twice was Gordon Cooper. His first flight was on the *Mercury/Atlas MA 9* on May 15, 1963, when he orbited Earth twenty-two times. His second trip was aboard the *Gemini/Titan 5* on June 3, 1965. During his two flights, Cooper logged 225 hours and 15 minutes in space.

Following a physical, a series of interviews, and further medical evaluations, a selection committee picks the applicants who are best suited for the job.

committee chooses applicants with the perfect blend of education, training, experience, and other unique skills that make them stand out from the crowd. Most important, successful applicants are team players—the type of people who can work well in a group in stressful situations.

The few applicants who make it to the very end get the job. They become "astronaut candidates" and are assigned to the astronaut office at NASA's

Johnson Space Center in Houston. There they participate in a challenging training and evaluation program designed to prepare them for missions to space and careers as full-fledged NASA astronauts.

So You Want to Be an Astronaut . . .

First step: Hit the books. Focus on science and math. Read every book about astronauts and space. Join clubs and teams and learn to work in a group.

In college, make good grades a priority. Majors like engineering, biological or physical sciences, and math are good choices. Try to land an internship in your field and work during the summers. Get your master's degree or, even better, a Ph.D. Once you have your graduate degree, you're ready to apply to NASA's Astronaut Candidate Training Program.

See you in space!

Training

When the aging John Glenn was selected for the 1998 *Discovery* mission, many experts doubted he could handle the physical challenge of astronaut training. Sure, he had blazed a path for modern space exploration with his daring orbital mission years ago, but this was different. Times had changed. Of course, he would eventually prove those doubters wrong, but first he had a date with the folks at the Johnson Space Center.

Basic training was brutal. To prepare for the event of disaster, Glenn learned to master emergency escape procedures—things like rappelling hundreds of feet from an escape hatch, parachuting to safety, and riding special baskets all the way down from the shuttle launch pad. He spent hours in a space shuttle simulator learning the ins and outs of the shuttle. He was outfitted with survival gear, including a life pre-server, an emergency supply of food and water, emergency oxygen bottles, and rescue beacons—things that would hopefully keep him alive should something go wrong.

Of course, this was just training. Glenn had yet to actually return to space. He wouldn't need to use

In preparation for his return to space, John Glenn uses a "sky genie" to simulate an escape from a troubled space shuttle.

Astronaut Profile

Karen L. Nyberg, Ph.D.,
Mission Specialist
Astronaut Candidate Program
Class of 2000
Born: October 7, 1969, Parkers
Prairie, Minnesota
Education: Henning Public
High School, Henning,
Minnesota, 1988; B.S.,
Mechanical Engineering,
University of North Dakota,
1994; M.S., Mechanical
Engineering, University of
Texas, 1996; Ph.D., Mechanical
Engineering, University of
Texas, 1998
Job: Environmental Control
Systems Engineer, NASA Johnson
Space Center, Houston, Texas

all this gear during practice, but he had better know how to use it when the real countdown began.

The Astronaut Candidate Program

Most astronauts begin preparing for space as members of NASA's Astronaut Candidate Program. There is a lot to learn about surviving in outer space.

Hitting the Books

One of the first things candidates do is take classes

designed to prepare them for space. Some classes cover the workings of the space shuttle. Others go through basic sciences—oceanography, geology, astronomy, mathematics, physics, and meteorology. Candidates learn how all those subjects apply to space and space flight. Finally, students learn how to navigate in space. Getting lost thousands of miles away from Earth could be fatal.

Formal training for space shuttle missions begins behind a desk. Candidates read manuals and use specialized computer software to learn about shuttle operation. They use single systems trainers to learn how to operate various parts of the orbiter, recognize malfunctions, and fix things when they go wrong.

Physical Demands

Sometimes, candidates have to prove they're in good physical shape before training can even begin. To ensure they're ready for underwater sessions that simulate what it's like to walk in space, candidates must pass a swimming test and learn how to scuba dive. The swim test is no simple lap in the pool. Candidates

Astronaut William Shepard is lifted to a helicopter during emergency-procedure training outside of Moscow.

have to swim seventy-five meters in a heavy flight suit and awkward tennis shoes, and tread water for at least ten minutes.

Candidates must also complete rigorous military survival courses on land and in the sea. They parachute into the ocean and spend hours bobbing in cold, choppy waters. They're strapped to harnesses and dragged face-first through dirt. They have to prove that they're capable of surviving anything.

Practice, Practice, Practice

Of course, one of the most important things for pilot astronauts to practice is flying, so they fly at least fifteen hours each month in NASA's T-38 two-seater jets. They also practice shuttle landings in a specially modified corporate jet aircraft designed to fly just like the real space shuttle. Mission specialists also put in flight time—at least four hours per month.

When trainees are ready, they board a modified KC-135 jet for space flight simulation. The jet includes many of the same types of equipment found in the space shuttle. It flies at such extreme speeds

Astronaut Profile

Terry W. Virts, Jr., Captain, U.S. Air Force, Pilot Astronaut Candidate Program Class of 2000
Born: December 1, 1967, Baltimore, Maryland
Education: Oakland Mills High School, Columbia, Missouri, 1985; B.S., Mathematics, U.S. Air Force Academy, 1989; M.A.S., Aeronautics, Embry-Riddle Aeronautical University, 1997
Job: F-16 Test Pilot, Edwards Air Force Base, California

and altitudes that passengers can, for a short period of time, experience what it's like to be weightless.

Pilots training for a mission to space can perfect their runway approaches and landings in modified business jets known as shuttle training aircrafts, or STAs. The jets perform just like the real orbiter.

Full-scale models of shuttle compartments allow astronauts to practice things like meal preparation and eating, storing equipment, managing trash, taking pictures with cameras, and conducting experiments. They also learn how to make an emergency exit once the shuttle lands.

Astronaut Jeffrey S. Ashby experiences a brief period of weightlessness during a flight on NASA's KC-125 "zero-gravity" aircraft.

Simulating Space

Because the atmosphere in space is nothing like it is on Earth, candidates learn to deal with extreme differences in atmospheric pressure. They spend time in what's called an altitude chamber, where atmospheric pressure can be adjusted to simulate what it's like in space. Extreme conditions—such as a sudden drop in pressure—can be created to help candidates train for emergencies.

NASA's Multifunction Electronic Display Subsystem (MEDS)—
"the glass cockpit"—will eventually be outfitted in all orbiters.

Using simulators outfitted with special training software, missions can be simulated from launch to landing. Crews experience what it's like to see stars out the orbiter windows. They even see a digital runway as they practice simulated landings.

The Shuttle Mission Simulator (SMS) allows candidates to experience what it's like inside the shuttle in the moments before the launch, during the ascent, and while in orbit. They learn how to work aboard the shuttle and perform the specialized maneuvers that might be required in space.

As the actual launch date nears, the astronauts' training picks up even more. They begin working

Virtual Reality

Thanks to relatively new high-tech developments at NASA's Ames Research Center in California, future space travelers can now strap in for liftoff, blast into orbit, and cruise to a safe landing—all within a model spacecraft that never leaves the building.

Today, scientists can do their work miles away from the flight simulators, using a handheld controller to "walk around" a three-dimensional, computerized world representing the test spacecraft. Known as "teleresearchers," they can even "enter" the training cockpit to see exactly what the astronaut-in-training sees, including controls, movement, launch pad, and landing strip.

with flight controllers in the Mission Control Center. A computer links SMS with Mission Control so everyone can communicate exactly as they would during a real mission. They learn to work together as a team and solve problems as they arise.

Other single systems trainers are used as well. Each trainer serves a specific purpose. The Neutral Buoyancy Laboratory, for example, is an enormous water tank. Astronauts enter the tank wearing pressurized space suits. Being underwater is similar to the feeling of weightlessness in space. A mock orbiter payload bay and airlock can be submerged in the pool. This allows astronauts wearing pressurized space suits to practice space walks.

The months—even years—of training inevitably pay off. Because the simulators allow future astronauts to see what space is like before they even get there, by the time they do go into orbit they have plenty of experience. In fact, many astronauts say the only major differences between their simulated missions and the real thing are the noise and vibration of real launches and the constant weightlessness experienced in space. Most missions are trouble free, so astronauts rarely have to use the emergency procedures they learned in training. Instead, they can focus on their jobs.

Strange New Worlds

Tuesday, January 28, 1986, was an incredibly dark day in the history of space exploration. Just seventy-three seconds into the flight of the space shuttle *Challenger*, something went terribly wrong. A booster rocket sprung a leak. Flames flew from the hole. Then, as millions of people around the world watched the televised event in horror, *Challenger* exploded.

Seven people died that day. Aboard the shuttle were Judy Resnik, an electrical engineer; Dick Scobee, the commander; Michael Smith, the pilot; Ellison Onizuka, an aerospace engineer; Ron McNair, a physicist; and Gregory Jarvis, a satellite engineer. One other passenger, a New Hampshire schoolteacher named Christa McAuliffe, planned to be the first teacher to ever travel into space. She hoped to deliver in-space lessons to millions of kids as the orbiter circled Earth.

Tragedy

The world was stunned. Over the previous decade, space travel had become all but routine. People thought it was only a matter of time before everyday citizens would fly to space like they flew to other countries. Accidents were unheard of.

NASA was stunned, too. The space agency was proud of its accomplishments and, until that tragic day, was sure of its continued success. At the urging of President Ronald Reagan's administration, NASA included a teacher on the shuttle—not because her presence was an absolute necessity for the success of the flight, but because she could renew the interest of the average citizen. McAuliffe would show the world what an amazing place space really was. She'd show that space travel was a challenge, but she'd also demonstrate that America was ready for the challenge.

On January 28, 1986, NASA experienced one of its darkest hours when seven people perished in the explosion of the space shuttle *Challenger*.

With the explosion of *Challenger,* all hopes were dashed. McAuliffe was dead. NASA was in trouble. It was suddenly clear that space flight wasn't as safe as everyone thought it was. The confidence that led NASA to try sending a citizen—a schoolteacher—into space was shattered.

Soon after, President Ronald Reagan delivered a speech. Acknowledging the brave astronauts who died in the accident, he said, "They had a hunger to explore the universe and discover its truths. They wished to serve, and they did—they served all of us. I know it's hard to understand that, sometimes, painful things like this happen. It's all part of the process of exploration and discovery; it's all part of taking a chance and expanding man's horizons."

Back to the Future

After the disaster, NASA took two years to launch another shuttle. During that time, aerospace engineers stayed hard at work, hoping to make future missions safer. And it appears they've done just that. There have been no other space shuttle fatalities since *Challenger*, even though more and more shuttles are launched each year. Today, more than fifteen years after the explosion, NASA's confidence is growing once again. The space agency hopes this safety record will continue, especially since they're hard at work on their latest project.

On the morning of September 8, 2000, the space shuttle *Atlantis* lifted off from Cape Canaveral, Florida.

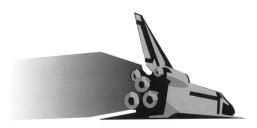

It was the ninety-ninth space shuttle launch in almost twenty years. The seven-member crew's mission: prepare the International Space Station for its first three long-term residents, scheduled to move in within months.

A space station is an orbiting scientific laboratory where astronauts can live and work in space. The atmosphere inside is controlled so that people can live safely without having to wear bulky space suits. The 140-foot-long International Space Station is more than 200 miles above Earth. NASA and other space agencies around the world hope it will become a permanent orbiting laboratory for space studies.

Astronaut Profile

John W. Young, NASA Astronaut
Born: September 24, 1930, San Francisco, California
Education: Orlando High School, Orlando, Florida; B.S., Aeronautical Engineering, Georgia Institute of Technology, 1952
Honors: More than ninety major awards, including the Congressional Space Medal of Honor (1981), the Rotary National Space Achievement Award (2000), and three NASA Distinguished Service Medals; member National Aviation and U.S. Astronaut Halls of Fame

On this mission, the crew's job was tough. They were to transfer more than two tons of supplies to the station. They also had a bit of technical work to do. An American astronaut, Ed Lu, and a Russian cosmonaut, Yuri Malenchenko, put on their space suits, left the shuttle, and floated toward the station's new control module. Once there, they hooked up cables, installed a navigation tool, and freed a jammed piece of equipment. Mission accomplished.

Vacation Hot Spots: The Bahamas, Hawaii . . . Mars?

It may sound crazy now, but one day in the not-so-distant future, there's a decent chance that everyday citizens—teachers, plumbers, doctors, firefighters—will have a new place to go on vacation: space. With a few technological twists and a couple of major financial turns, Mars, Mercury, and the Moon could become hotter destinations than the Bahamas or Hawaii.

This artist's rendition of a possible mission to Mars depicts explorers stopping to inspect a robotic lander and its small rover.

Sound unlikely? Well, maybe. But some experts think it's only a matter of time before humans can fly to space like they jet from state to state or between countries. And in fact, some innovative companies are banking on it. An aeronautics company in Denver, Colorado, for example, hopes to put 100 people on Mars by 2030. Another company plans to build an enormous floating space station that can be used to house vacationing guests—an orbiting hotel, so to speak.

Unfortunately, there are some problems that have to be overcome before space vacations become a reality. The temperature on Mercury, for example, is 620°F—too hot even for sunbathers. Another issue is the price: A space station would cost billions of dollars to build.

So don't pack your bags just yet. For now your best ticket to space may be as a professional astronaut. But if your ambitions of piloting the space shuttle don't work out, never fear. A journey to space—if only for the holidays—may not be such a long shot after all.

Life in Space

W hen working in space, astronauts have to take special safety precautions. Because there is no atmospheric pressure or oxygen in space, they must wear special suits during space walks. Space suits are designed to supply oxygen for breathing and to keep the atmospheric pressure similar to that of Earth. Space suits also serve as a protective barrier between astronauts and deadly flying objects like micrometeorite. Minor punctures can be dealt with on the fly with a repair kit, but a major collision, something that has never happened before, could be fatal.

Solar and cosmic radiation are other space hazards. The ultraviolet radiation from the Sun is at an extremely

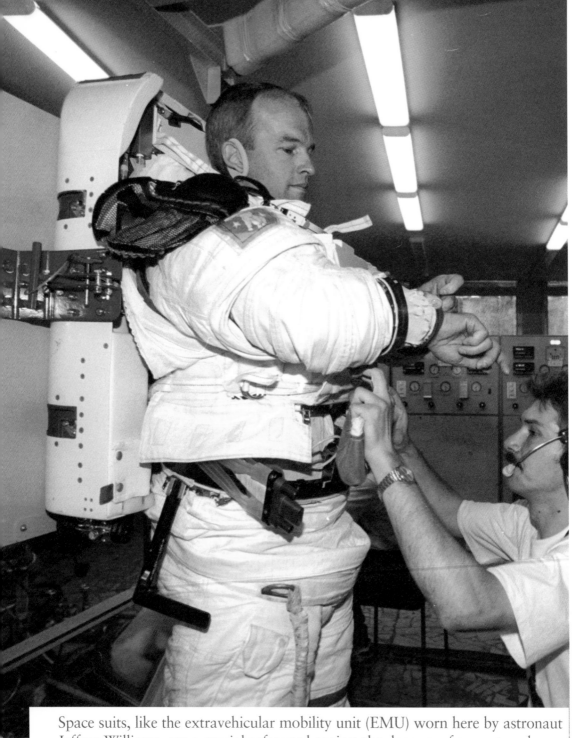

Space suits, like the extravehicular mobility unit (EMU) worn here by astronaut Jeffrey Williams, are a crucial safeguard against the dangers of space travel.

high level because in space there is no protective atmosphere like there is over Earth. Space suits protect astronauts from this radiation, and special tinted visors shield their eyes. Suits also keep astronauts insulated from the extreme temperatures of space.

Space is a dangerous place. Astronauts know that. That's why they train so hard on Earth before they launch into orbit. They want to be prepared in the event something—anything—goes wrong.

Mir

Most of the time, thanks to space-age technology and training, space missions are trouble free. Astronauts go to space, do their work, and return to Earth without a hitch.

So on June 25, 1997, when news came that there was a serious problem aboard the Russian space station *Mir*, many people were shocked. Things had gone terribly wrong. And the lives of three people—one American astronaut and two Russian cosmonauts—were in extreme danger.

The Russian space station *Mir* orbits Earth above the Pacific Ocean during rendezvous operations with the space shuttle *Discovery* on February 6, 1995.

The *Mir* space station had had a long history of problems. Sent into orbit in 1986, the aging ship had since experienced a faulty oxygen system, leaks in its cooling system, and a fire. Each accident had forced *Mir*'s Russian cosmonauts and visiting American astronauts to do in-space emergency repairs. Those aboard *Mir* had grown used to facing problems in space. But nothing prepared them for what happened next.

U.S. astronaut Michael Foale and his Russian crewmates, Vasily Tsibliyev and Alexander Lazutkin,

had a mission: Using remote control, they had to steer an unmanned Russian resupply ship to a safe docking with *Mir*. Normally the crew would have used an electronic guidance system to help them guide the craft, but thanks to a limited budget, they couldn't afford such a system and were forced to do the docking entirely by hand.

As Tsibliyev, the Russian commander, maneuvered the joysticks that controlled the cargo vessel's approach, it suddenly became apparent the supply ship was moving too fast. From the station's core module,

Tsibliyev fired the resupply vehicle's thrusters, hoping to reverse its direction. It was too late.

"I felt a big thud," Foale recalled in an interview shortly after the accident. "My next thought was . . . Is this going to kill us immediately or do we have time?"

Two hundred miles above Earth, *Mir* was suddenly wounded. The eight-ton resupply vehicle had missed the docking port and smashed into the space station's *Spektr* science module, where Foale did his scientific

Astronauts Michael Foale *(left)* and Russian cosmonaut Vasily Tsibliyev communicate with their families from the *Mir* space station in July 1997.

experiments. The impact put a hole in the module's hull and knocked *Mir* into an out-of-control spin.

For the crew, the hole in the ship was the first major concern. They were losing pressure as the station's atmosphere was sucked into space. As their ears popped, they realized their oxygen was disappearing fast.

Fortunately, the leak was small. The crew had time. As Foale prepared an escape vehicle, Lazutkin worked to seal the hatch that led to the punctured *Spektr* module. Eventually, the hatch was sealed. Then, to replace the air that had been lost, the crew opened a tank of pure oxygen in the station's main module. The station's pressure went back to normal.

Character and Courage

"Part of our character as Americans is that we are by nature explorers and adventurers. Along with that adventure and exploration goes risk. But it's a risk that we accept. For if we ever give up being explorers, then we have lost part of the character of the American people."
—Astronaut and former U.S. Representative Bill Nelson, speaking on the tenth anniversary of the space shuttle *Challenger* explosion.

Mission Control operatives on the ground work with the astronauts in space to ensure a smooth-running operation.

But there was another problem. Because the station was spinning, *Mir*'s huge, energy-producing solar panels were not in the right position to capture sunlight. There was no power. And without power, controls aboard the station were useless. The crew could do nothing but watch the stars.

Luckily, Foale had an idea. By watching the stars go by, he calculated how fast *Mir* was tumbling. The crew was still in radio contact with Mission Control, so they relayed their calculations down to Earth.

Mission Control then used a remote-control command to start *Mir*'s engines.

It worked. Gradually, the spinning station came to a stop. But there were still problems. *Mir* had stopped in a position with its solar panels in shadow, so there was still no power aboard the ship. Without power, they could do nothing.

But the crew had another idea. The thrusters from the spacecraft they used to get to the station might be powerful enough to push *Mir* into position. Tsibliyev crawled into the craft, started its engines, and fired away. Amazingly, *Mir* tilted just enough to capture the Sun. The lights came back on, motors started, and instruments returned to life. Finally, they were back in action.

Hacked

When it comes to technology, NASA is on the cutting edge. In fact, they have to be—otherwise, sending spacecraft and astronauts into orbit would be impossible. Day in and day out, NASA scientists use computers and other high-tech gadgetry to ensure that missions are a success and astronauts remain safe. But even so, sometimes things go wrong.

Another near-catastrophe took place in 1997. As a space shuttle docked with the Russian space station *Mir*, a computer hacker tapped into NASA's communications system. For a brief moment, contact between NASA professionals on the ground and the astronauts in the shuttle was impossible.

Fortunately, NASA was quick to fix the problem and reestablish communications. But this incident made it clear how easily a criminal with the right technological tools could endanger the lives of those in space. "It shows the potential hackers have for doing some real damage to NASA's mission and astronaut safety," said NASA inspector general Roberta Gross.

Space Colonization

According to NASA, there's a good chance that colonization of space—especially of Mars—will take place during your lifetime. In fact, the International Space Station should be completed by 2002. NASA

Manned missions to places like Mars,
while feasible, are still years away.

also hopes to send manned exploratory missions to Mars at some point, but for now those missions are still in the planning stages.

Assuming we do establish a small colony of humans in space, it will most likely be underground—at least at first. Because the Martian atmosphere is so thin, exposure to particle bombardment and radiation from space would be a problem—a very dangerous one—for the first inhabitants. Living underground would provide protection and safety. Light will have to be generated beneath the Martian soil, using solar collectors, or generated by a nuclear reactor. Food, of course, is hard to come by on Mars, so people would have to figure out a way to grow their own crops, most likely through the use of special greenhouses.

The creation of true space communities is still years away, but if NASA has anything to do with it, the day will come.

Touchdown

When astronauts have completed their work in space, they must focus on getting back home. But it's not as simple as cruising back on autopilot. The crew has a lot of work to do to prepare the shuttle for return. On their last full day in orbit, they have to clean up their living area, stow all equipment, and do some last-minute calculating and figuring for the people back at the space center.

A shuttle mission is not successful until the orbiter touches down on the runway.

The crew has a deorbit preparation handbook to make sure they cover the major events leading up to touchdown. They have to get the go-ahead from Mission Control to close the payload bay doors. The shuttle must be positioned tail-first to slow down its speed and force. Then it must be turned around so that it will reenter Earth's atmosphere nose-first. Because of the high heat of the atmosphere,

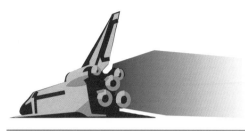

Please Write

Thanks to the nature of their job, astronauts are very popular and have a lot of fans. But they're also very busy people. Still, if you want to contact an astronaut, the best way to do so is through a written letter. Address it to:

Astronaut's Name
c/o Astronaut Office/CB
NASA
Johnson Space Center
Houston, TX 77058

Who knows? If you're lucky, maybe he or she will write back.

communication with Earth is temporarily interrupted on reentry. About twenty miles from touchdown, the shuttle zeroes in on an alignment circle 18,000 feet in radius. It sharply slopes toward the ground and finally, at speeds of over 200 mph, touches down on the space center runway.

Mission accomplished.

Timeline

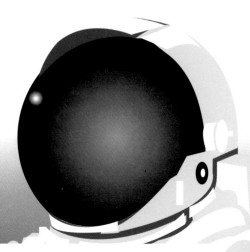

1957 The Soviet Union launches *Sputnik 1*, the first artificial satellite in space. Later, *Sputnik 2* is sent into orbit with a passenger: a dog named Laika, which lives for seven days, proving that animals can survive in space.

1961 Soviet cosmonaut Yuri Gagarin, aboard *Vostok 1*, becomes the first person to orbit Earth. Later, Alan Shepard, aboard *Freedom 7*, becomes the first American to go to space.

1962 John Glenn is the first American to orbit Earth.

1963 Cosmonaut Valentina Tereshkova is the first woman in space.

1965 Cosmonaut Aleksei Leonov takes the first tethered space walk.

Astronauts: Life Exploring Outer Space

1966 *Gemini 8*, piloted by Neil Armstrong and David Scott, connects with an Agena rocket stage for the first successful vehicle-to-vehicle docking in space.

1967 The *Apollo 1* command module bursts into flames during a test on the launch pad at Cape Kennedy, Florida. Astronauts Virgil Grissom, Ed White, and Roger Chaffee are killed in the fire.

1968 *Apollo 8* is the first manned spacecraft to orbit the Moon.

1969 Neil Armstrong and Edwin "Buzz" Aldrin leave *Apollo 11* to become the first humans to walk on the Moon.

1970 An oxygen tank in the *Apollo 13* service module ruptures, forcing the crew to abort their mission and return to Earth.

1971 A crew of cosmonauts returning from the first space station, *Salyut 1*, are killed when their spacecraft becomes depressurized during reentry.

1981 The space shuttle *Columbia* is launched. Many more space shuttle missions follow.

1983 Sally Ride becomes the first American woman astronaut.

1984 Astronauts Bruce McCandless and Robert Stewart use backpacks fitted with special jet engines to take the first untethered space walks.

1986 *Challenger* explodes, killing all seven crew members. The Soviet space station *Mir* is launched.

1995 After spending a record 437 days, 18 hours in space aboard *Mir*, cosmonaut Valery Polyakov returns to Earth.

1998 Former senator John Glenn flies to space for a second time aboard the space shuttle *Discovery*. Construction of the International Space Station begins.

2002 The International Space Station is scheduled for completion.

Glossary

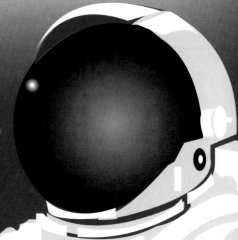

ascent   An upward movement.

astronaut   A person who trains for space flight or travels in space.

astronaut pilot   Space shuttle commander or pilot.

astronomy   The study of objects and matter found in space.

atmosphere   Layers of gas that surround a star or planet.

command module   A space vehicle designed to carry the crew, communications equipment, and equipment necessary for return to Earth.

cosmonaut   A Russian astronaut.

countdown   A backward counting that marks the time remaining before a launch.

deploy To move an object into its appropriate position.

descent A downward movement.

docking The manual or remote-control connecting of spacecraft in space.

extravehicular activity (EVA) Human activity, such as a space walk, that takes place in space but outside a spacecraft.

gravity A force of attraction between two objects influenced by their mass and the distance between them.

International Space Station A permanent orbiting space laboratory scheduled for completion in 2002.

launch pad A structure from which spacecraft are launched into space.

liftoff The moment when a spacecraft leaves the launch pad and begins its journey to space.

micrometeorite A very small rock or piece of dust in space.

mission specialist Astronaut responsible for helping the commander and pilot and coordinating in-space experiments and payload operations.

National Aeronautics and Space Administration (NASA) The government agency that oversees the U.S. space program.

Astronauts: Life Exploring Outer Space

Neutral Buoyancy Laboratory   An enormous pool of water used by astronauts to train for work in the weightless environment of space.

orbit   The path followed by a planet, satellite, space-craft, or any other object in space as it revolves around another object, like Earth.

payload   The important supplies and equipment carried by a spacecraft and necessary to the mission.

payload bay   The main compartment of the space shuttle where the payload is kept.

payload specialist   An astronaut with specialized scientific or technical skills brought along to conduct experiments with the payload or perform technical work.

reentry   The moment when a spacecraft reenters Earth's atmosphere after travel in space.

Remote Manipulator System (RMS)   A mechanical arm on the space shuttle used by astronauts to move objects in and out of the spacecraft.

satellite   Any object that orbits Earth, the Moon, or other body in space.

Shuttle Mission Simulator (SMS)   A computerized training device that imitates the space shuttle and allows astronauts to practice launch, flight, and landing operations.

simulator Man-made device that creates a space-like environment and allows astronauts to practice before they get to space.

space The region beyond Earth's atmosphere.

space walk To leave a spacecraft and step into space while wearing a space suit.

thruster A spacecraft engine used to control the craft's position while it's in space.

touchdown The landing of a spacecraft on Earth after a mission.

For More Information

Astronaut Hall of Fame
6225 Vectorspace Boulevard
Titusville, FL 32780
(321) 269-6100
Web site: http://www.astronauts.org

The Astronauts Memorial Foundation
The Center for Space Education
Mail Code AMF
State Road 405, Building M6-306
Kennedy Space Center, FL 32899
(321) 452-2887
Web site: http://www.amfcse.org

**National Aeronautics and Space Administration
(NASA) Headquarters**
300 E Street SW
Washington, DC 20546-0001
(202) 358-0000
Web site: http://www.nasa.gov

National Space Society
600 Pennsylvania Avenue SE
Suite 201
Washington, DC 20003
(202) 543-1900
Web site: http://www.nss.org

**U.S. Space Camp, Space Academy, and
Aviation Challenge**
U.S. Space and Rocket Center
One Tranquility Base
Huntsville, AL 35807-7015
(800) 63-SPACE (637-7223) or (205) 837-3400
Web site: http://www.spacecamp.com

The Young Astronaut Council
5200 27th Street NW

Washington, DC 20015
(202) 682-1984
Web site: http://www.yac.org

WEB SITES

The Astronaut Connection
   http://www.nauts.com
NASA Goddard Space Flight Center
   http://www.gsfc.nasa.gov
NASA Jobs
   http://www.nasajobs.nasa.gov
NASA Kids
   http://kids.msfc.nasa.gov
NASA Spacelink
   http://spacelink.nasa.gov
NASA Space Society
   http://www.ari.net/nss

For Further Reading

Baird, Anne. *Space Camp: The Great Adventure for NASA Hopefuls.* New York: Morrow Junior Books, 1992.

Berliner, Don. *Living in Space.* Minneapolis, MN: The Lerner Publications Co., 1993.

Burch, Jonathan. *Living Dangerously: Astronauts.* Ada, OK: Garrett Educational Corporation, 1992.

Cole, Michael D. *Astronauts: Training for Space.* Springfield, NJ: Enslow Publishers, 1999.

Cole, Michael D. *Columbia: First Flight of the Space Shuttle.* Springfield, NJ: Enslow Publishers, 1995.

Cole, Michael D. *Space Emergency: Astronauts in Danger.* Springfield, NJ: Enslow Publishers, 2000.

Landau, Elaine. *Space Disasters.* New York: Franklin Watts, Inc., 1999.

Astronauts: Life Exploring Outer Space

Maze, Stephanie. *I Want to Be—an Astronaut*. San Diego: Harcourt Brace & Company, 1997.

Ride, Sally, and Susan Okie. *To Space and Back*. New York: Lothrup, Lee & Shepard, 1986.

Stott, Carole, and Clint Twist. *Space Facts*. New York: DK Publishing, Inc., 1995.

Wolfe, Tom. *The Right Stuff*. New York: Bantam Books, 1983.

Index

Astronauts: Life Exploring Outer Space

About the Author

Chris Hayhurst is a freelance writer living in northern Colorado.

Photo Credits

Cover © NASA; p. 6 © SuperStock; pp. 9, 13, 29, © Corbis; pp. 11, 14, 23, 24, 33, 36, 45 © NASA; p. 17 © NASA/Joe McNally, *National Geographic*; pp. 20, 38–39, 40, 42 © AP Worldwide Photo; p. 47 © Reuters New Media, Inc./Corbis.

The Rosen Publishing Group would like to thank and acknowledge NASA and Mike Gentry for their photo contributions to this book.

Design and Layout

Les Kanturek